Develop
A Player

How to Play the Position of
Number 8
(No.8)

Disclaimer

The information in this book is meant to supplement, not replace, proper rugby union training. Like any sport involving speed, equipment, balance and environmental factors, playing the sport of rugby poses some inherent risks. The authors and publisher advise readers to take full responsibility for their safety and know their limits. Before practicing the skills described in this book, be sure your equipment is well- maintained and do not take risks beyond your level of experience, aptitude, training or comfort level.

Copyright

Purpose

The purpose of this book is to provide the player, family, coach and player's support network with the information needed for positional excellence in the position of **Number 8 (No. 8)** in rugby union.

Objectives

The objectives of this book are:

☑ To provide the reader with an understanding of the natural physical and mental development of young players in the sport of rugby union.

☑ To explain the demands of rugby union and use that information to help guide the player's development.

☑ To provide a blueprint for the core conditioning needed to achieve results in the game of rugby union.

☑ To provide an insight into what selectors and coaches are looking for at a representative level.

☑ To provide FREE access to a professional player development portal **www.developaplayer.com** whereby the player can record and share their rugby development with friends, family, coaches, sponsors and selectors.

Table Of Contents

Chapter 1:
Understanding emotional and physical development

Overview

In this chapter you will gain knowledge of the following:

- ☑ **Background**
- ☑ **How an athlete's brain works**
- ☑ **The role of natural testosterone in sports development**

Background

The brain is an amazing thing. An athlete who wants to be the best they can be in a sport they love is equally as amazing. Both need to be understood, nurtured and allowed to develop over time.

By understanding the brain, the player, coach, and supportive family members can help both the brain and the player achieve truly awesome things.

The brain grows like a tub of sprouts left in the sun. Brain cells get longer and make new connections. The left half of the cortex grows slower than the right in all human babies, but in males, it develops over a longer period, with the female hormone oestrogen promoting faster growth in girls than boys. As the right half of the cortex grows, it tries to make connections with the left half. In boys, the left half of the brain isn't ready to make the connection. After reaching out to the left and being unable to plug in, the right half stays where it is.

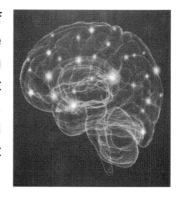

As a result, the right half of a boy's brain is richer in internal connections but poorer in cross connections to the other half of the brain. It is therefore clear that regular practice actually helps the brain's connections to connect permanently, so encouragement and teaching affect the shape and power of the brain in later life. So why is this important to know?

How the rugby brain works

Our brains are brilliant and flexible devices that are always learning. Parents normally teach a young boy how to avoid getting into fights and how to solve disputes peacefully, reinforcing that knocking someone over is not tolerated.

Coaches, who aren't aware of the brain's development, ask these same young developing players to forget all those early social rules, so delicately taught, and demand that they go out onto the field of play and be a dynamic and unstoppable rugby sensation.

Some boys are ready for this challenge and take to it like a duck to water, however to other this can be challenging and therefore need a little more time, and a little more nurturing from their parents and coaches before they are ready to compete to the fullest of their ability.

At these early stages of a young man's rugby career we can normally identify four types of rugby players.

- Type 1 – The "Thinker" who eats, breathes and sleeps rugby.
- Type 2 – The "Bulldozer" who loves the physical game.
- Type 3 – The "Star" who is expected to be playing rugby.
- Type 4 – The "Developing" kid who is not yet sure why he is playing rugby.

The role of natural testosterone in sports development

Testosterone in varying degrees affects every boy. It gives a boy growth spurts, makes him want to be active, and makes him competitive.

Testosterone triggers significant changes:

- Around the age of 4 – Initial activity and boyishness

3

- Around the age of 12 – In rapid growth and disorientation
- Around the age of 14 – Is testing limits and breaking through to early manhood

The boy with testosterone in his bloodstream likes to know who the boss is, but also wants to be treated fairly. Bad environments bring out the worst in him. The boy with lots of testosterone needs strong guidance and a safe, ordered environment to help him develop his rugby ability and leadership is needed to channel his rugby enthusiasm productively.

Boys need to learn empathy and feeling, and be shown tenderness if they are to progress in life's journey. As the rugby player develops he does not need ridicule and blame from his parents or coach. It is important that these role models provide understanding and support. It is our job to honour and steer a young man in a healthy direction if he is to become a well-rounded rugby player for the future.

There is hope for all the four types of rugby players as natural windows of accelerated developmental exist which the player, parent and coach should be mindful of and be ready to take fully advantage of in the pursuit of sporting excellence. Chapter 8 takes a look at these developmental windows in greater detail

Chapter 2:
The four disciplines of great rugby

Overview

In this chapter you will gain knowledge of the following:

- ☑ **Attacking rugby**
- ☑ **Defensive rugby**
- ☑ **Physical conditioning**
- ☑ **Mental conditioning**
- ☑ **The influencers on the four disciplines**

Background

In the modern era of rugby union, there is considerable emphasis put on size, strength, genetic make-up and aggression. This emphasis is detrimental to the young player.

It is true that at the highest level of professional rugby and international competition, size does matter. Gone are the days when front row players had a certain shape, second row players were the tallest on the field and wingers were speedsters with little or nothing in the way of bulk muscle.

That being said, there are exceptions to size. If we look deeper than just the physical appearance we can see the journey these players have been on which led them to become the top players in their current positions.

Rugby union is seen by many as a complicated game of massive collisions, infringements, stoppages and periods of no action. Others see the sport as a strategic movement of players in complex formations achieving superiority in numbers in certain regions of the pitch, which leads to scoring opportunities. Both perspectives can be true, but there are a multitude of additional interpretations in-between.

We need to help young players entering the game of rugby union understand that the game is actually one to be enjoyed. We need to help them understand it is a game of strategy, evasion and the core disciplines of attack and defence, but also of physical and mental conditioning. If the young athletes can understand these aspects and execute them with pace, power, agility and skill, then irrespective of their size, strength or genetic make-up, they can compete at the highest level of rugby union and reap the emotional and social benefits of success.

Attacking rugby

Attacking rugby can be broken down into two scenarios; when you have the ball in your possession and when you don't.

Attacking with the ball in possession

When you have the ball in your possession you have the advantage. Sometimes young players' forget that and start to panic, which leads to mistakes in running, passing and catching.

If you are attacking with the ball, then the opposition needs to react and try to stop you. If you can attack quicker, with greater skill and more purpose, the outcome will be positive.

The ability to attack with confidence stems from three simple building blocks:

- Attack space (knowledge)
- Know you can execute a skill with confidence and precision (practice)
- Keep focused and be in the moment (commitment)

Attacking without the ball in possession

Due to the fluidity of the game, the conditioning, and the number of players on the field, the support role of team members in attack is equally as essential as the primary attacking player himself.

In younger age groups, if a player breaks through a tackle line they tend to run the length of the playing area and score. However, as the size of the playing area and the number of players on the field increases, the defence tends to regroup, meaning that attacking without the ball in possession is equally as important.

The ability to attack without the ball in position, therefore, comes down to three key aspects:

- Anticipating where the likely contact point with the defence will be and be in position to keep the attacking movement going (support)
- Providing options for attacking continuity (understanding)
- Decide what the best role will be in providing those support options for attacking continuity (be a team player)

Defensive rugby

Defensive play has evolved dramatically in recent times, primarily down to the influence of other sports. Defensive structures, defensive roles, and defensive policies have all played a major part in the modern game of rugby union, leading to more strategic thought on how to break down those defensive patterns.

It is important to also understand where attacking sides are most likely to score, and then develop a defensive policy in response, but not at the expense of the natural skills and flair of players being able to defend instinctively.

To understand how and when to defend effectively statistical analysis is very important. If we look at the 2014 statistics information from the southern hemisphere Super 16 sides where tries were scored some interesting insights can be drawn.

Team	From own lineout	From own scrum	From restart receipts	From open play - tap	From kick receipts	From turnovers
Blues	23	13	12	4	28	19
Brumbies	25	6	15	1	34	19
Bulls	23	9	12	2	33	21
Cheetahs	22	5	12	5	34	22
Chiefs	18	12	13	4	29	24
Crusaders	20	10	14	2	36	18
Highlanders	18	11	13	3	33	22
Hurricanes	16	11	14	3	33	23
Lions	25	10	13	3	26	22
Rebels	21	13	13	4	31	19
Reds	24	12	10	3	29	23
Sharks	21	9	13	2	36	20
Stormers	22	11	10	2	33	20
Waratahs	19	13	15	4	27	23
W-Force	22	12	10	3	33	21

Average	21	10	13	3	32	21

From reviewing this kind of data we can start to identify insights on what to defend and why thereby providing a competitive edge over the opposition. For example, if we were to use the above data to develop our defensive policy we could conclude that if a team was to defend well from kick receipts, lineouts and turnovers, then they would have statistically reduced the attacking sides' probability of scoring by 74%.

We can, therefore, look at defence principles associated with set pieces and broken play to become more effective in this part of the game.

Defending set pieces

Set pieces are defined as either lineouts or scrums. Based on the statistics identified above, we would break each down into the elements and put in place defensive practices that would focus on the following:

- **Lineout Defence** – Look to defend the following areas:
    - At the point of catch in the lineout
    - On the short side of the lineout (between the touch line and the 5M line)
    - On the immediate open side of the lineout (between the 15m line and the goal posts)

- o On the far open side (between the goal posts and the opposite touch line)
- **Scrum Defence** – Look to defend the following areas:
  - o Defend the scrum by not retreating
  - o Within 2m of the scrum (both sides)
  - o Within 15m of the scrum (both sides

By looking at these specific aspects of set piece play we are identifying defensive channels. By understanding these channels, defensive patterns can be developed and adapted to counter sides that are more likely to attack from set pieces.

Defending broken play

Broken play defence is defined as either defending from when the ball has been kicked to the attacking team, or when the attacking team has maintained possession after a contact situation. By using the playing statistics identified earlier we would again look at defensive policies around the following:

- **Restart Receipts** – Look to defend the following areas:
  - o Within 10m of the attacker receiving the ball (to prevent momentum)
  - o Behind the first defensive line (in case of a line break)

- o Deep (in case of chips, grubbers and territory advantage)
- **Tap** – Look to defend the following areas:
  - o Within 10m of the attacker receiving the ball (to prevent momentum)
  - o Within 15m of the tap (to prevent early line breaks)
- **Kick Receipts** – Look to defend the following areas:
  - o Within 10m of the attacker receiving the ball (to prevent momentum)
  - o Behind the first defensive line (in case of a line break)
  - o Deep (in case of chips, grubbers and territory advantage)
- **Turnovers** – Look to defend the following areas:
  - o Within 1m of the turnover (to counter pick and go)
  - o Within 3m of the turnover (to counter first receiver)
  - o Within 5m of the turnover (to counter first receiver running onto the ball at pace)

Physical conditioning

Young rugby union players should find enjoyment in the game and be able to compete, and therefor a certain level of base conditioning is a very important factor that allows them to do so.

A typical length of a rugby field is 100m for the field of play plus the depth of the in-goal areas at both ends of the field, say 10m each - total 120m. The width is typically 70m so the area = 120m x 70m = 8400 sq m. A full size pitch (22m in-goal) would be 144m x 70m = 10080 sq m

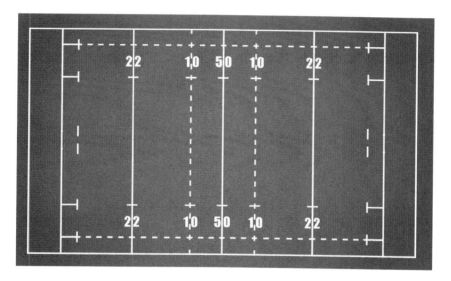

Being able to run is essential. Rugby, after all, rugby is an active game, and to be able to enjoy the game, the young athlete must have a sufficient base level of physical conditioning to be able to compete for the duration of each match.

- **Under 6s'**
  - o Field size = 50m x 25m
  - o Playing time = 10 minute haves
  - o Playing numbers = 7 per side
- **Under 7s'**
  - o Field size = 50m x 25m
  - o Playing time = 15 minute haves
  - o Playing numbers = 7 per side
- **Under 8s' and U9s'**
  - o Field size = 70m x 35m (half field)
  - o Playing time = 15 minute haves (20 minutes for U9s'
  - o Playing numbers = 7 per side (10 per side for U9s')
- **Under 10s' and 11s'**
  - o Field size = 120m x 65m
  - o Playing time = 20 minute haves
  - o Playing numbers = 12 per side
- **Under 12s'**
  - o Field size = 120m x 70m
  - o Playing time = 25 minute haves
  - o Playing numbers = 15 per side
- **Under 13's to Under 19s'**
  - o Field size = 120m x 70m
  - o Playing time = 35 minute haves
  - o Playing numbers = 15 per side

When considering the dynamics and body movements of a rugby player, it is interesting to know that the average distance a forward runs with the ball in hand during a game is between 5 to 10 meters in any one carry and that a back normally runs on average between 10 to 30 meters. That doesn't seem like a lot and, in fact, it isn't when compared to athletics where kids run hundreds, if not thousands of meters in a single athletic race.

Rugby union, however, is unique in that it requires forwards and backs to perform those relatively short distances when the ball is in hand at 100% output, reload, and then go again. Additionally, the sport requires the player to be operating at 60-70% of their maximum in support and then be able to immediately reach that 100% output the moment they have the ball in hand.

By understanding these dynamics, we can put in place the necessary conditioning that will help rugby athletes have the physical stamina necessary to perform in these attack and defence scenarios.

General Physical conditioning

To get an idea of the general physical conditioning levels needed to perform in a particular playing position at a particular age, the Develop A Player organization has mapped out a number of range parameters as a guide aligned to two commonly used tests which are further explained in Chapter 3. Additional, and specific physical conditioning for different playing positions is outlined in Chapter 4, which provides a deeper understanding of the conditioning needed for great rugby.

- Recommended conditioning test 1 - Multi-stage Fitness Test (Bleep Test) for aerobic endurance
- Recommended conditioning test 2 - 30m Sprint Fatigue Power Maintenance Test for speed and power

Mental conditioning

Sports play a huge role in our society, and as such mental conditioning needs to be taken seriously as it can play a huge role in helping athletes achieve success. Participation in childhood sports can be a rewarding experience and a good introduction can lead to a lifetime of enjoyment.

For parents, coaches and support networks, understanding who understand mental development in young players can increase the player's overall involvement and enjoyment of sports. As the adults guiding children in sports, it is important for them to remember that, while there are some fundamental building blocks for success, no two people are completely alike.

Understanding a child's development helps adults avoid unnecessary frustration and inappropriate expectations while simultaneously creating an environment of learning, increased participation, and fun.

Young children (ages 7-10 years) face two major challenges in sports:

- Learning how to get along with friends
- Learning how to interact with authority figures other than their parents

At this young age, learning to cooperate within a team and compromising for the interests of someone else are major accomplishments. Children at this young stage of a sport are just beginning to develop the ability to see the world from the perspective of others. Parents and coaches should make a clear distinction between what is acceptable behavior and what is not. Since the child is learning, we need to provide them with the opportunity to grow through guided trial and error. It is important to remember that fun, exploration, and developing a love of sports are key elements at this age. If competition and winning become the main themes, these are most likely fostered by adults, which means they should temper their competitive nature in the interests of the child.

Pre-adolescents (ages 10-13 years) face the social challenges of developing best friends and gaining acceptance from peers. Social relationships are one of the developmental milestones that this age group is navigating. They want to be part of a group and often fear being embarrassed. Developing a same-sex best friend is a major task of this social stage. Pre-teens tend to be loyal to their friends and make many decisions based on maintaining their friendships. "Sports hopping" is an example of a decision based on maintaining a friendship. Sports hopping occurs when a pre-teen changes sports or quits participating in sports because of friendships.

During the pre-teen phase of development, practices should be structured that allow for social interactions. Coaches often view social interactions at practices as 'goof off' time. Contrary to many coaches' beliefs, a practice which contains structured social interaction as part of a regular routine helps develop team relationships.

Adolescents (ages 14-18 years) face the developmental challenge of defining who they are and how they fit into the world. Identity development is a complex process that involves applying the training and teaching we have given them, while the teen is trying on different identities. The teen is attempting to discover who they are and clarify their values through exploring different facets of their personality. This process occurs as parents and coaches wring their hands and watch as their own hair turns gray in exasperation!

Often, we see the teen's identity search in the clothes they wear, the music they listen to, and the changes they make in who their peers are. Being tolerant of the adolescent while they try out new ideas is an important behavior for parents and coaches. Tolerance for new behaviors is guided by the rules that the behaviors do not place the teen in danger or interfere with team rules and goals. The second major transition during the teenage phase is recognizing that sports is truly important in life.

The teen makes the transition in identity from 'I play rugby' to 'I am a rugby player.' Participation in sports and being an athlete becomes a significant piece of their identity. Helping the teenage athlete enhance the technical mastery of their chosen sport while supporting their growth as an individual, is a challenge facing both parents and coaches.

Regardless of an athlete's age, there are several common themes that relate to participation in the sport that should be considered;

- To have fun
- For fitness
- Being with friends
- To compete

The social aspect of sports and having fun is appealing to the young athlete. Competition or winning is not the predominant motivator.

Recognizing the young athlete's need for encouragement, socialization, and fun is paramount. If the young athlete develops a love of sports, then with support and a healthy coaching environment, the drive for competition and mastery naturally develops.

No matter the age of your young athlete, there are several simple keys that help sports participation and competition evolve naturally:

- Be supportive.
- Avoid TMTS (Too Much Too Soon); children's natural drive for competition will evolve as they age.
- Structure time to include social interaction and fun.
- Help your teen incorporate athletics as part of their identity by being   positive.

The influencers on the four disciplines

Fathers, mothers & care givers

Sports should be fun for kids. Treat sport as a game, it is not a business for kids.

With all the money in professional sports today, it is hard for parents to understand that it is just good fun to young athletes. The primary goal should be to have fun and enjoy the healthy competition.

Young athletes' compete in sports for many reasons. They enjoy the competition, like the social aspect, engage with being part of a team, and enjoy the challenge of setting goals. Parents and coaches may have a different agenda than your young athlete, and as such they need to recognize that it is their sport, and not that of the parent or coach.

Emphasize a mental focus on the process of execution instead of results or trophies. We live in a society that focuses on results and winning, but winning comes from working the process and enjoying the results. Teach your young athlete to focus on the process of the challenge of playing one shot, one tackle, or one run at a time instead of the number of wins or trophies.

Parents and coaches are role models for young athletes'. As such, you should model composure and poise on the sidelines. When you are at a competition, your young athlete will mimic your behavior as well as other role models. You become a role model in how you react to a close race or the questionable behavior of a competitor or official. Stay calm, composed, and in control during games so your young athlete can mimic those positive behaviors.

What are some of the things parents can do to help their kids enjoy and succeed at sports?

5 Rules for supportive parents and care givers

1. Do what you can to make sure your child is having a positive experience with coaches and teammates. The wrong coach can turn a kid off to a sport. Similarly, conflicts with teammates and peer pressure can make sports quite unpleasant. Help your child work out these interpersonal issues. In some instances, you may need to intervene or intercede on his behalf.

2. Try to determine if your child seems better suited for team sports or for individual sports. Some kids love the camaraderie of team sports. Others enjoy competing on their own. And of course, some kids like both.

3. Be sure to model good sportsmanship, grace, gentleness, and integrity on and off the athletic field. If you behave inappropriately at training and matches, your children are likely to do the same.

4. Lots of kids have difficulty managing busy schedules, which include games, practices, travel, family activities and school work. In many instances, the parents and their kids are spread quite thin and can easily become overwhelmed. Help your child find a balance and make sure they

do not have too much on their plates at any one time.

5. Be aware of burn out. If your child has lost some of their enthusiasm and their performance has declined, your youngster may be burnt out. Talk with them to see if they need a break, a new challenge, or a different approach to their sport.

Coaches

Take the time to reflect on why it is you coach. This is beneficial not only for personal growth but also in creating an awareness of changes in our motivation.

- Motivation (why we do what we do) affects our behaviour (what it is we do).

Therefore, changes in our motivation can be reflected in our behaviours and also in our wellbeing.

Research suggests that coaching for intrinsic reasons such as love, joy and passion is associated with better outcomes. These outcomes include the health and wellbeing of the coach, improved coach-athlete relationships, athlete motivation, satisfaction, and performance.

Three psychological needs have been identified as important in fostering greater intrinsic motivation for an activity. To what degree do you feel these needs are satisfied by your coaching work?

- The need for autonomy (the desire to feel that your actions emanate from your own choice)
- The need for competence (the desire to be good at the activity)
- The need for relatedness (the desire to be connected to others)

Those who feel they coach because they want to, are good at it. Coaching allows them to continue relationships within their sport and with their athletes, display more intrinsic motivation for coaching, and coach with a more autonomy-supportive style.

Therefore, being aware of why you coach your sport is an important and reflective practice.

Your coaching motivation plays a crucial role in the facilitation of a healthy coaching environment, both physically and psychologically. Working in an environment that supports your needs will help you get the best out of yourself as well as your athletes.

Sports coaches assist athletes in developing to their full potential. They are responsible for training athletes in a sport by analyzing their performances, instructing in relevant skills, and by providing encouragement. But you are also responsible for the guidance of the athlete in life and in their chosen sport.

Consequently, the roles of the coach will be many and varied, and range from instructor, assessor, friend, mentor, facilitator, chauffeur, demonstrator, adviser, supporter, fact finder, motivator, counselor, organizer, planner, and even the fountain of all knowledge.

In relation to sports, the role of the coach is to create the right conditions for learning and to find ways of motivating the athletes. For athletes who are already highly motivated, the task is to maintain that motivation and generate excitement and enthusiasm.

The coach will need to be able to: assist athletes in preparing training programs, communicate effectively with athletes, assist athletes in developing new skills and use evaluation tests to monitor training progress and predict performance.

The role of the coach can be seen as a very difficult task requiring a very special person, and therefore, they need to be ready to perform in this role.

Chapter 3:
General conditioning for the modern game

Overview

In this chapter you will gain knowledge of the following:

- ☑ **The science behind rugby conditioning**
- ☑ **Conditioning tests and performance ranges**

Background

There are different thoughts on how to undertake the right conditioning for young players and there are loads of online resources that can be used to undertake the conditioning evaluation.

In this chapter the most useful tests relevant to young players has been identified, how to undertake those tests and what the expected performance ranges per age group should be.

Firstly, this book does not recommend any weight training for young players in any rugby position until about 15 years of age, as the muscles, tendons, and bones are still growing and require careful management if the player is to enjoy later years of development and injury-free playing.

The recommended baseline tests are to assess aerobic endurance, power, and speed.

The science behind rugby conditioning

As a child grows, his nervous system becomes more mature. With this maturity, the child becomes more and more capable of performing increasingly complex actions. The rate at which these motor skills emerge is sometimes a worry for parents. Caregivers frequently fret about whether or not their children are developing these skills at a normal rate. As mentioned above, rates may vary somewhat, however, nearly all children begin to exhibit these motor skills at a fairly consistent rate unless some type of disability is present.

There are two types of motor skills:

- **Gross** (or large) motor skills involve the larger muscles including the arms and legs. Actions requiring gross motor skills include walking, running, balance and coordination. When evaluating gross motor skills, the factors that experts look at include strength, muscle tone, movement quality and the range of movement.
- **Fine** (or small) motor skills involve the smaller muscles in the fingers, toes, eyes and other areas. The actions that require fine motor skills tend to be more intricate, such as drawing, writing, grasping objects, throwing, waving and catching.

27

Physical development in children follows a directional pattern:

- **Large muscles** - develop before small muscles. Muscles in the body's core, legs and arms develop before those in the fingers and hands. Children learn how to perform gross (or large) motor skills such as walking before they learn to perform fine (or small) motor skills such as drawing.
- **The center** - of the body develops before the outer regions. Muscles located at the core of the body become stronger and develop sooner than those in the feet and hands.

Conditional tests and performance ranges

There are many conditioning tests available to coaches and selectors to evaluate a player's current and future suitability in a sport, or indeed, to a particular position either at the representative or elite level.

Some prefer a series of detailed evaluations taking metrics of: speed and quickness, strength and power, agility and flexibility, and some prefer the more simple approach of taking a player's height and weight at a certain age and then using the parents height and weight as an indication of what the young athlete will attain once fully matured.

Some of the main tests used are identified below with the recommended two highlighted:

Fitness Component	Evaluation Test
Anaerobic Endurance	Running-based Anaerobic Sprint Test
Aerobic Endurance	Multistage Fitness Test or Bleep test - **Recommended**
Agility	Illinois agility run test
Balance	Standing Stork Test Blind
Body Composition	Body Fat Percentage
Coordination	Hand Eye coordination
Fitness General	Wilf Paish Rugby Football Tests
Flexibility	Sit and Reach test
Psychology	Sport Competition Anxiety Test
Reaction Time	Ruler Drop Test
Strength - Core	Core muscle strength and stability test
Strength - Elastic	Standing Long Jump test
Strength - General	Burpee Test
Speed and Power	30 M Sprint Fatigue Power Maintenance Test - **Recommended**
Aerobic Endurance	Yo-Yo (Stage 1) and Yo-Yo (Stage 2)
Aerobic Endurance	300M endurance run

Recommended baseline test 1 for aerobic endurance

Multistage Fitness Test (Bleep Test) - The Multistage Fitness Test, more commonly known as the Bleep Test has been around for many years and, as such, good data exists to draw comparisons from.

How to run baseline test 1

This test requires the athlete to run 20m in time with a beep from a CD recording. The athlete must place one foot on or beyond the 20m marker at the end of each shuttle.

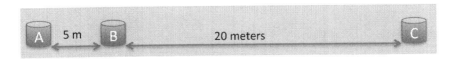

- When signaled by the CD the athlete runs from cone C to cone B.
- The athlete continues running between the cones as signaled by the CD.
- The assistant keeps a record of each completed lap
- A warning is given when the athlete does not complete a successful out and back shuttle (cone B to C and back to B) in the allocated time, the next time the athlete does not complete a successful shuttle the test is stopped.

- The assistant records the total distance completed.

The below is a table broken down by age and performance level for the bleep test:

Age	Excellent	Above Average	Average	Below Average	Poor
6 - 8	N/a	N/a	N/a	N/a	N/a
8 - 10	N/a	N/a	N/a	N/a	N/a
10 - 12	L8 S9	L7 S1	L6 S6	L6 S1	< L5 S3
12 - 14	L11 S2	L8 S9	L7 S1	L6 S6	< L6 S1
14 - 16	L12 S7	L11 S2	L8 S9	L7 S1	< L6 S6
17 - 20	L12 S12	L11 S6	L9 S2	L7 S6	< L7 S3
21 - 30	L12 S12	L11 S7	L9 S3	L7 S8	< L7 S5
31 - 40	L11 S7	L10 S4	L6 S10	L6 S7	< L6 S4
41 - 50	L10 S4	L9 S4	L6 S9	L5 S9	< L5 S2

Recommended baseline test 2 for power and speed

30m Sprint Fatigue Power Maintenance Test requires the athlete to complete 10 x 30m sprints.

How to run baseline test 2

- The athlete warms up for 10 minutes.
- The assistant sets up the course as per the diagram opposite using the cones.
- The assistant gives the command "GO" and starts the stopwatch.
- The athlete sprints from A to B between the cones deviating 5m sideways in the middle of the sprint.
- The assistant stops the stopwatch when the athlete's torso crosses the finish line at B and records the time.
- The athlete jogs slowly back to point A (taking

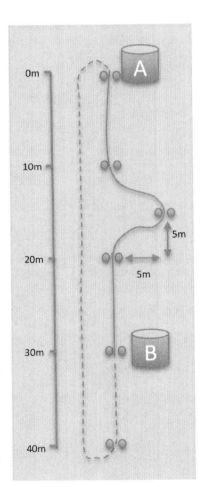

32

no longer than 30 seconds to do so) following the route on the diagram.

- The athlete is to complete a total of 10 sprints from A to B and the assistant is to record the times.
- Determine the average speed of the first three trials and divide it by the average speed of the last three trials.

Calculation Example

- 1st Set of 3 = 7.1s, 6.9s, 6.9s;
- 2nd Set of 4 = 7.0s, 7.2s, 7.1s, 7.3s;
- 3rd Set of 3 = 7.3s, 7.4s, 7.5s

The average of the first 3 times (7.1s, 6.9s, 6.9s) = 6.97s and the average of the last 3 times (7.3s, 7.4s, 7.5s) = 7.4s

Power Maintenance = 6.97s / 7.4s = 0.94

The table below is broken down by age and performance level for the Sprint Fatigue Power Maintenance Test:

Age	Excellent	Above Average	Average	Below Average	Poor
6 - 8	N/a	N/a	N/a	N/a	N/a
8 - 10	N/a	N/a	N/a	N/a	N/a
10 - 12	>89%	85-89%	80-84%	75-79%	<75%
12 - 14	>89%	85-89%	80-84%	75-79%	<75%
14 - 16	>89%	85-89%	80-84%	75-79%	<75%
17 - 20	>89%	85-89%	80-84%	75-79%	<75%
21 - 30	>89%	85-89%	80-84%	75-79%	<75%
31 - 40	>89%	85-89%	80-84%	75-79%	<75%
41 - 50	N/a	N/a	N/a	N/a	N/a

Chapter 4:
How to play the position of Number 8
(No. 8)

Overview

In this chapter you will gain knowledge of the following:

- ☑ **The Number 8's role at the lineout**
- ☑ **The Number 8's role at the scrum**
- ☑ **The Number 8's role in open play**

Background

The Number 8 Player is one of the most influential playing positions on the field. He plays a linking role between the forwards and the backs and as such must be a supreme tactician of the game. The Number 8 should be capable of putting in massive tackles, making hard yards through contact situations and get involved in open play rugby.

The Number 8 will often be one of the most skillful players of the forwards possessing excellent ball handling skills, strong mental strength and even be capable of kicking the ball effectively if required.

The Number 8 Player will combine the height of the Blindside flanker and the muscular build of a prop. Most modern Number 8's are usually around 190cm tall and weighing around 110Kg. This means that the Number 8 is large enough to be a crucial ball carrying threat to the opposition while at the same time the athleticism to be a jumper in the lineout. It is also vital for the Number 8 to be incredibly fit so that they can get around the field and involve himself in all aspects of the game.

In defence, the Number 8 has an essential role to play putting in substantial defensive tackles to bring down the opposition ball carriers effectively and the added ability to compete in the ruck to turn over the ball. Setting strong defensive structures is also a vital attribute of the Number 8, being able to defend close around the breakdown as well as knowing defensive structures in the back line.

In attack, the Number 8 has two principal roles in open play attacking rugby.

- **Ball carrier** - The Number 8 must be a strong carrier of the ball with the ability take the ball into contact and retain possession.
- **Playmaker** - The Number 8 must be able to spot weaknesses or mismatches in the opposition defensive structures and be able to exploit these by either taking the ball into contact or setting up players to take advantages of these identified weaknesses.

When the ball is in the opposition half of the field, the Number 8 will have to decide to either fully commit to the attacking movement or hold back with the fullback and the wingers to form a new attacking movement if the opposition attempt to make a clearing kick.

The Number 8's role at the lineout

The Number 8 normally takes up a lineout position second from the back ready to be the jumper on a long throw-in option to the back. Catching the ball at the back of the lineout has some strategic choices. As the ball is already 15 meters in from the sideline meaning there are attacking options both down the short side, I.e., between the back of the line and the nearest touch line, and the opportunity to quickly attack the opposition Outside-half around the back of the lineout.

By being one of the more athletic and robust members of the team, the Number 8 is equally comfortable with either being the primary jumper or to be a lifter of another teammate when it is his team's throw in at the set piece.

On the oppositions throw in the Number 8 has a variety of options in defence and how to put pressure on the opposition. He can either compete in the air for the ball; he can compete once the opposition has won the ball but still held within the lineout, or he may choose to hold his position and exert pressure on the opposition's backline attack if the ball is moved wide.

There is a train of thought that says you need to practice a movement 10,000 times before it becomes an automatic physical action of the body. Whereas there is not necessarily the need to practice a lineout 10,000 before the Number 8 is proficient in this area, there is a need for the developing player to become familiar with this part of the game. Sloppy practice does not help any player develop, however with concentration and commitment to this aspect of the game an active Number 8 can have a dramatic impact on the success of the lineout in both attack and defence.

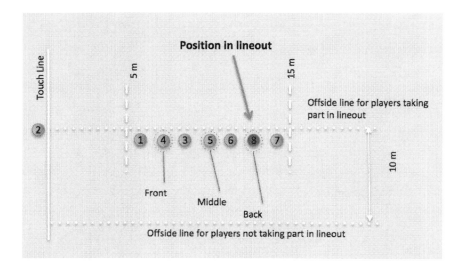

- **Front throw** - A throw to the front of the lineout must be delivered as the jumper is getting into the air, the ball is primarily won at this position due to superior speed and reaction time. The Number 8 would be one of the supporters for this lineout option.

- **Middle throw** - A throw to the middle is made just as the jumper starts to jump, therefore timing is essential as there is likely to be opposition jumpers that need to be avoided. The Number 8 would be one of the supporters for this lineout option.

- **Back throw** - A throw to the back is usually made as the back jumper starts to move and thus the ball is in flight before the jumper has started to rise. The Number 8 would be a primary jumper for this lineout option.

The Number 8's role at the scrum

The Number 8 packs down at the back of the scrum between the Loose-lock and the Tight-lock. His primary role is to hold the two locks together while at the same time adding his weight and force to the forward drive of the scum.

In attack, I.e., when it is the Number 8's team that puts the ball into the scrum, the ball will be hooked by the Hooker, and the ball will arrive at the feet of the locks. It is the Number 8's role to either use his feet to bring the ball all the way to the back of the scrum so that the Scrum-half can pass the ball away from the base of the scrum or the Number 8 must continue to drive the scrum forward until the ball arrives at his feet. The Number 8 may also choose to pick the ball up himself from the back of the scrum and break to either the left or the right of the scrum. This attacking option is usually pre-arranged with the Scrum-half with the intention of getting over the gain line as quickly as possible and initiate an attacking move that sees his team gain excellent field position, or even it can lead directly to a try-scoring opportunity.

In a defensive scrum, the Number 8 has to be a great tactician and a reader of the opposition's body language. If the Number 8 believes that the opposition is looking just to hook the ball back and move the ball away from the scrum, then he can put all his effort, and considerable size, into pushing in the scrum in an attempt to disrupt the opposition gaining clean, quick ball.   If he, however, believes that there is a set move planned between the Scrum-half and the opposition Number 8 / Blindside winger then he needs to be mindful of the role he will need to be performing in defence.

Should the opposition Number 8 or Scrum-half pick the ball up and attack near to the scrum then the Number 8 will most likely be the second line of defence as either the Openside flanker or the Blindside flanker will have made the initial tackle. The Number 8 will then have to make a split second decision to either compete for the ball, in an attempt to turn over the possession or to position himself ready for the next attacking movement.

Scrum binding

The binding of the Number 8, if not done correctly can dramatically disrupt the ability of the scrum.

As stated in Rugby Union Laws of the Game Section 20.3 part (f).

"All players in a scrum, other than front-row players, must bind on a lock's body with at least one arm prior to the scrum engagement. The locks must bind with the props in

41

front of them. No other player other than a prop may hold an opponent."

However it should be noted that as per the U19 variations Law 20.3 part (f) states:

"Binding between the legs of either prop by either locks is illegal"

Body position and the tower of power

When it comes to feet position in the scrum, whether it is to push off one foot or two, to pre-bind with the locks or not, there is no one correct answer. There is a multitude of different variations and options for different scenarios all of which need to be studied, observed, practiced and perfected.

There is, however, universal agreement that if the Number 8 can achieve an effective pushing position in the scrum, then his team gets a significant advantage over the opposition.

The key is power generation. Therefore an effective Number 8 should work with all the other members of the forwards to achieve the best possible body position and superior pushing technique to generate collective power generation. We generate power by pushing the grass back with our toes and straightening our legs in a forward, not up, movement. To do this, we keep our knees parallel to the ground and our legs in contact with the ground. Our hips move forward by straightening our legs and keeping our backsides low. The focus is on having both feet in connection with the field for the maximum amount of time and only moving the feet forward once the full leg extension has been completed.

The body position for the most effective driving movement is referred to as the 'tower of power' and is broken down into the following parts:

- Feet slightly wider than shoulder width.
- Balls of the feet firmly on the ground and leaning forward.
- An angle of 120 degrees between the calf and the leg.
- Hips pivot backwards and chest comes forward.
- Bend at the hips.
- Flat back.
- Head in a neutral position and eyes looking through the eyebrows.

43

- Clench teeth and push the tongue to the roof of your mouth.
- After the engage ensure the hips have moved forward.

Forward force

The focus for the Number 8 should be to keep the scrum square and moving forward.

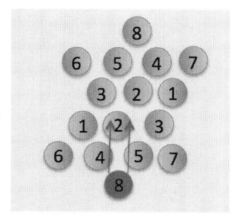

He should be mindful of a break by the opposition down the blind-side as well as an open-side attack therefore he needs to be an expert at both the scrum and a solid defender.

Synchronization / timing

Getting all the eight forward in the scrum to work in unison can be challenging. Props and Hookers are competing for the best position in the front row, employing all the subtle skills of the 'dark arts' and associated shenanigans! The locks are focused on generating power, and the flankers are balancing the job of providing support to the props while at the same time scanning the opposition for attacking opportunities and defensive needs.

In the modern day scrum, the combined weight of all eight forward can be approximately 850kg. If all the members of the scrum can, therefore, push in the same direction, at the same time, with excellent body position and superior technique, then scrum dominance can be achieved. If scum dominance can be achieved, then that can have a dramatic impact on the game.

Many coaches teach an engagement call and following count such as "hit....1,2,3" to focus the players into a unison push. There is a lot of merit in teaching this to developing players on the understanding that the call is ultimately designed to apply tightness of the scrummaging pack and pressure on the opposition.

The goal

The goal of the synchronization and timing, and resulting tightness and pressure is ultimately to apply sufficient force on the opposition pack to force them to give up their good body shape. If the opposition props and hooker are unable to maintain their good body shape, then the scrummaging power lines are disrupted leading to a disintegration of their scrummaging capability. Once this happens then the strategic advantage in the game is achieved.

This is why coaches put such a massive emphasis on 'win the engagement, and you will win the scrum". If the Number 8 can contribute to winning the engagement and maintain good and strong body shape, then the chances of delivering a stable platform from which his Scrum-half can mount an effective attacking movement is achieved. Alternatively, if the Number 8 can help achieve dominance in the scrum for his side, then the physical and psychological advantage is achieved.

The Number 8's role in open play

The pivotal role of the Number 8 in open play is so varied in the modern game of rugby that we would need to write multiple chapters on field movements, positioning, shapes, structures, defensive policies and a deep understanding of all the various backline attacking patterns.

To gain the essential understanding of the skills needed to perform well in the position of Number 8, we will just focus on the three main areas of Number 8 play which are the breakdown, the scrum restart and the running lines of the Number 8 and the linking role of the Number 8.

The Number 8 at the breakdown

Competing at the breakdown to secure ball possession, and maintain the continuity and flow of the game is one of the primary jobs of the Number 8. Having a player that can compete well in multiple rucks in quick succession gives the Number 8's team ball security. Ball security leads to pressure on the opposition, and pressure on the opposition leads to points in terms of scoring tries or successful penalty kicks. Whereas the Number 8 may not score as many tries as other players on the field his role at the breakdown will be the reason behind the team's success.

Typically the Number 8 will arrive at the breakdown just behind the flankers and so must have a good understanding of the breakdown laws. He must make a split second decision to either compete for the ball or take up a position ready for the next passage of play.

At the breakdown, there are some roles the Number 8 can adopt.

- **The Jackle** - This is the person who is practiced at regaining the ball from the opposition by either ripping it off then while the ball is off the ground or have the superior technique that would enable him to re-gather the ball once it has gone to ground.
- **The Pest** - This is the role taken up by the Number 8 when the ball is on the ground waiting for the next phase of play. By attacking the breakdown, and disrupting the ability of the opposition to recycle the ball quickly, the

objective is achieved which is to give his team an extra few seconds to set the defensive structures around the breakdown.

- **The disruptor** - this is a similar role to the pest but with the intention not just to slow down the recycling of the ball, but to look to cause a turnover of possession. By driving hard into the breakdown, the Number 8 is looking to cause a handling error or create the need for the opposition to commit additional players to the breakdown thus reducing the number of attack options for the next phase of play.

In each of the three roles of jackle, pest or disruptor, the core fundamentals of excellent breakdown technique are the same which are: footwork, balance, and player removal :

The 1,2,3 of great breakdown technique

1. When approaching the breakdown keep your head and shoulders low, but above your waist. Look to get your shoulders below that of the opposition player you are looking to clear out. The best way to prepare for the contact is to bend from your waist so that your spine stays straight which gives you power and then getting your leading foot as close to the opposition player as possible (footwork)

2. As you make contact, ensure that your shoulder engages first on or below his waist of the opposition player. By making contact in this area of the opponent's body, you disrupt their natural centre of balance. By disrupting their balance, you gain the upper hand.

3. Once contact is made, with the balance of the opposition player impacted, you use momentum to remove the player out of the breakdown competition. Take control of the opponent and use leg drive to remove the player up and to the left, or up and to the right to remove the opposition from the breakdown in a backward manner. Alternatively, use your body weight to bring the player down and to the left, or right, if you need to remove the player in a forward direction.

The Number 8's lines of running

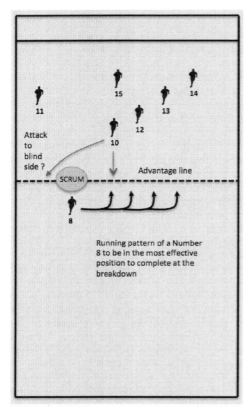

Attack to blind side ?

SCRUM

Advantage line

Running pattern of a Number 8 to be in the most effective position to complete at the breakdown

From a scrum restart, the Number 8 will normally not arrive at the resulting breakdown until immediately after the first tackle.

Since the Number 8 needs to be jumping in the lineout, competing in the scrums, making tackles all over the field and carrying the ball strongly into contact, the efficiency of the Number 8's lines of run from the scrum is extremely important so that he conserves energy.

Although many sides operate various defensive systems such as a 'rush defence' or a 'drift defence pattern, the path that the number Number 8 takes usually remains the same . He needs to run what is referred to as a "J" line which means he makes a tracking line and then turns to face forward at the end before the next phase commences. This allows him to view the evolving play, looking to plug any gaps in the defensive structure and take any necessary action needed.

When contact is made he is then in the correct position to legally comment to the breakdown in one of the roles of jackler, pest or disruptor.

The linking role of the Number 8

When not competing for the ball at the breakdown the Number 8 plays an instrumental role is setting the defensive shapes around the breakdown, therefore, must have an excellent understanding of the game and have the mental strength to lead other players. The Number 8 also needs to be a good passer of the ball as he will often play the linking role putting other ball carriers into space. He will need to practice filling in for the Scrum-half on occasion as well so will need to have a good understanding of the back line patterns and set moves.

Chapter 5:
Additional conditioning for the position of Number 8

Overview

In this chapter you will gain knowledge of the following:

- ☑ **Number 8 conditioning for the lineout.**
- ☑ **Number 8 conditioning for the scrum.**
- ☑ **Number 8 conditioning for open play.**

Background

The Number 8 should be one of the most competitive players in the team as well as a master tactician of the game. He will never give up, even the most challenging circumstances, and will never settle for second place. This attitude is essential if he is to fulfill his role successfully and a deep understanding of the game is vital.

He will be a thinker of the game, able to understand the principles of attack and have the physical strength and stamina to be able to be effective.

A Number 8 is mainly in close contact situation, scrums, rucks, mauls, lineouts etc. The Number 8 must therefore develop strength and skills to be effective under these conditions. The Number 8 must work hard at their absolute strength levels to provide the power in the scrum, the athletic ability in the lineout and close contact situations. Handling, evasion and passing are essential elements of the modern back-row.

Number 8 conditioning for the lineout

For the modern Number 8 to be effective in the lineout, he needs to possess athletic, explosive, and dynamic power with a sound understanding of the various tactics of lineout strategy.

Modern Number 8's at the top level can weigh up to 110kg so great core, and all over body strength are essential to cope with the high-impact, repeat effort scenarios of the modern game.

Where the Number 8 is the jumper in the lineout, he needs to possess excellent ball handling skills to either deliver the ball securely to the Scrum-half or to have the strength to take the ball forward under close contact scenarios.

To jump efficiently in the lineout, the Number 8 needs to take full advantage of plyometric training. Plyometric training utilises the elastic energy of the body's tissues, exploiting the stretch reflex at high-speed to achieve supreme lineout jump capabilities.

Key aspects for lineout conditioning	Why
Range of movement	Moderate range of movement at the hips, knee and ankle, lots of movement at the shoulder
Muscle used	Lower body: quadriceps, bottom, hamstrings, calves Upper body: deltoids
Time available to apply force	Short, fraction of a second
Amount and direction of force produced	Moderate (owing to the speed), vertical
Movement speed	Fast
Muscle contraction type	Eccentric, isometric and concentric with a high degree of muscle stretch and reactivity

Box jump drill for leg strength

- Place a sturdy structure directly in front of you.
- Bend at the knees and spring upwards and
- forwards.
- Use the arms to drive upwards and forwards.
- Land with both feet on the box, bending the knees to take the force

Medicine ball push for explosive power

- Use a medicine ball of sufficient weight.
- Start in a low squat position.
- Drive upwards quickly pushing the ball up and as high at possible.
- Tense the core throughout the movement and catch the ball as it rebounds off the wall.

Number 8 conditioning for the scrum

To be effective in the open the Number 8 needs to develop fantastic strength and power as well as being fast and athletic. The following weekly work out is therefore suggested.

Engage	Duration	Intensity	Repetition
Direct Engage (attack)	10 seconds hold	100% output for duration	5 reps
Direct Engage (hold)	15 seconds hold	70% output for 10 seconds then 100%output for 5 seconds	5 reps
Second Effort	15 seconds hold	100% for 5s; 70% for 5s; 100% for 5s	5 reps

Additionally, there are numerous position specific drills that can be done. Four great drills are as follows

- **Drill 1: Ball lift:** Two players bind with right arms and each use their left hand to pick up a ball between them. They then have to put it down. Change binding and hands. Make the players move to different points to pick up and put down a ball.
- **Drill 2: All four corners:** Two players bind together in a small grid with 4 different coloured cones on the corners. Starting in the middle the players move from cone to cone on the orders of the coach, whilst maintaining the same axis they started on. This will

mean for- wards, backwards and sideways movements.

- **Drill 3: Front row limbo dancing:** Two players hold a pole (e.g. flag post) at hip height. Two players bind and then "walk" sideways under the pole. Lower the pole depending on the success.

Number 8 conditioning for open play

To be effective in the open the Number 8 needs to develop fantastic strength and power as well as being fast and athletic. The following weekly work out is therefore suggested.

Development	Exercise
Leg Strength	• Knees to chest • Hurdle jumps
Upper Body Strength	• Clap chest push ups • Medicine ball slam downs • Medicine ball throws to the wall

Speed	• **Pyramid sets (four rounds)**
	   ○ 1x100m, 2x75m, 3x50m, 4x25m
	• **Six by forty (six rounds)**
	   ○ Sprint 40m with a slow walk back in between each rep

Acceleration	• **Twenty fives (four rounds)**

	o Slow jog for 25m then sprint at maximum output for 25m with a slow jog back in between each rep • **Five meter swerve (four rounds)** o Sprint hard for 5m hard cut diagonal for 5m then push hard off other foot to straighten for another 5m

Conditioning	• **Fifty meter sprints (ten rounds)**
	  o Sprint 50m then slow down and walk to other end of the field, turn and go again
	• **The Malcolm Drill (ten rounds)**
	  o Start lying face down on half way line get up back pedal to 10m line go down on chest get up and run through to opposite 10m line go down on chest get up and back pedal to half way line and go down, that is one rep

Chapter 6:
The essential knowledge for developing great rugby

Overview

In this chapter you will gain knowledge of the following:

- ☑ **Young player development**
- ☑ **Catch and pass skills development**
- ☑ **Tackling skills development**
- ☑ **Breakdown skills development**

Young player development

Children go through predictable growth periods known as developmental milestones. These milestones are broken into main areas of development.

- **Cognitive Development** - This is the child's ability to learn and solve problems. For example, this includes a two-month-old baby learning to explore the environment with hands or eyes.
- **Social and Emotional Development** - This is the child's ability to interact with others, including helping themselves and self-control. Examples of this type of development would include a boy knowing how to take turns in games at school.

- **Fine Motor Skill Development** - This is the child's ability to use small muscles, specifically their hands and fingers, to pick up small objects, hold a spoon, turn pages in a book, or use a crayon to draw.
- **Speech and Language Development** - This is the child's ability to both understand and use language. For example, this includes a 12-month-old baby saying his first words and a two-year-old naming parts of his body.

Why is it important to know these things if we are developing rugby players? Well, if we know how a young player develops from ages six into adulthood, we can adjust our speech, words, drills, and attitude to ensuring that players have a positive experience in the sport of rugby union.

Catch and pass skills development

To become competent in the sport of rugby union, a developing player needs to learn how to catch and pass the ball at a proficient level and to work within the team environment. To do this effectively the developing player needs to learn five types of basic passing.

1. **Basic pass** - This is a very versatile pass that can be used in many situations. It allows you to easily control the speed and distance of the pass.
2. **Long clearing pass** - This pass is used most often when you are the Scrum-half or the player acting in that role. You remove the ball from the base of the scrum or a ruck and send it out to the backs. If you position your feet and arms well in relation to the ball, you can pass swiftly, giving the receiver more time and space.
3. **Close support pass** - You use two hands for this pass; gentle and soft to close players. Move your arms to disguise what you are doing, but supply power mainly with your fingers, giving great control over short distances.
4. **Get out of trouble pass** - Useful when a long ground pass is required but you are not in the correct position to make one and are being pressured which prevents you from taking time to get set. A risky pass. Should only be attempted by the highly skilled in dire emergencies.
5. **Over head pass** - You use this pass to get the ball to a supporting player when there is an opposition player directly between you and your support. The lobbing motion allows the ball to travel in an arc above and out of reach of your opponent(s).

Tackling skills development

Tackling is one of the absolute fundamentals of rugby and as such needs to be learned, re-enforced and continuously worked upon during a player's career. If the technique is learned safely and thoroughly at an early age, then that player will always be able to execute the skill and take joy from that part of the game.

Front on tackle (passive)

This tackle is commonly referred to as the sacrifice tackle. If perfected, it will be achieved every time, regardless of the opponent's size, height, and strength.

To successfully execute this technique the following process is followed

- Imagine the target on the bottom of the ball carrier's shorts.
- When tackling, keep the head up and with the chin of the chest.
- Brace the shoulders.
- Make initial contact with shoulders on the ball carrier's thigh.
- Keep the arms around the carrier's legs.

- Keep the head up and to one side of the ball carrier's legs.
- Use momentum to take the ball carrier over the shoulder.
- Twist around and land on top of the tackled player.
- Get up immediately after the tackle and compete for the ball.
- The child's ability to use small muscles, specifically their hands and fingers, to pick up small objects, hold a spoon, turn pages in a book, or use a crayon to draw.

Front on tackle (active)

The objective of this tackle is to drive the ball carrier behind the advantage line. To successfully execute this technique the following process is followed:

- Get the lead foot as close as possible to the ball carrier.
- Keep eyes on the point of contact.
- Keep head to one side.
- Drop hips to lower the centre of gravity.
- Drive shoulder up to the centre of the target either into the stomach or onto the chest.
- Power comes from an explosive drive upwards emanating from the legs and buttocks.
- Wrap the arms around the player.

- If possible pick one leg up.
- Keep driving until the attacking player's balance is broken and you are in control of his body.
- Continue forward landing onto of the attacking player.
- Get up immediately after the tackle and compete for the ball.

Side on tackle

This kind of tackle requires the tackler to anticipate the future point of contact and then track the ball carrier. Once the tackler has positioned the ball carrier into the desired position, then the following process should be followed:

- Get the lead foot as close as possible to the ball carrier.
- Imagine the target on the bottom of the ball carrier's shorts.
- When tackling, keep the head up and with the chin of the chest.
- Brace the shoulders.
- Make initial contact with shoulders on the ball carrier's thigh.
- Keep the arms around the carrier's legs.
- Keep the head up and to one side of the ball carrier's legs.

- Use momentum to take the ball carrier over the shoulder.
- Twist around and land on top of the tackled player.
- Get up immediately after the tackle and compete for the ball.

Rear tackle

This tackle requires the tackler to anticipate the future point of contact and possess an attitude that means he never gives up. A rear tackle is normally used when an attacker has broken the gain line and is heading for the try line. It's not so much about ability, it's about attitude and commitment. Once the tackler has got close enough to the ball carrier, then the following process should be followed:

- Get the lead foot as close as possible to the ball carrier.
- Imagine the target on the bottom of the ball carrier's shorts.
- When tackling keep the head up and with the chin of the chest.
- Brace the shoulders.
- Make initial contact with shoulders on the ball carrier's thigh.

- Keep the arms around the carrier's legs.
- Keep the head up and to one side of the ball carrier's legs.
- Drive with the legs, gripping with arms and hands to bring the ball carrier to the ground.
- Land on top of the tackled player.
- Get up immediately after the tackle and compete for the ball.

Smother tackle

The idea of the smother tackle is to wrap the ball carrier up so that he can neither pass the ball nor release the ball. This kind of tackle should be taught to players who are already proficient in the other forms of tackling rather than use it as the primary tackle technique. To successfully execute this technique the following process is followed:

- Get the lead foot as close as possible to the ball carrier.
- Keep eyes on the point of contact.
- Wrap the arms around the upper part of the ball carrier's body.
- Trap the ball and the player's arms.
- Add your own weight to the ball carrier and bring the player to the ground.
- Land on top of the tackled player.

66

Breakdown skills development

A breakdown happens when there is a stop in the forward momentum but the ball is still live and in active play. The three scenarios where this happens are as follows:

- **Tackle** - Only the ball carrier can be tackled by an opposing player. A tackle occurs when the ball carrier is held by one or more opponents and is brought to the ground, i.e. has one or both knees on the ground, is sitting on the ground or is on top of another player who is on the ground. To maintain the continuity of the game, the ball carrier must release the ball immediately after the tackle, the tackler must release the ball carrier and both players must roll away from the ball. This allows other players to come in and contest for the ball, thereby starting a new phase of play.

67

- **Ruck** - A ruck is formed if the ball is on the ground and one or more players from each team are on their feet close around it. Players must not handle the ball in the ruck, and must use their feet to move the ball or drive over it so that it emerges at the team's hindmost foot, at which point it can be picked up.

- **Maul** – When the ball carrier is held, but not brought to the ground, a maul may be formed. For a maul to form there must be at least three players involved, including the ball carrier, an opponent holding the ball carrier, and a team mate of the ball carrier bound to the ball carrier. When a maul has formed, it must keep moving forward towards a goal-line. The players must stay on their feet. Once a maul has been formed, an offside line comes into force for both teams which is parallel to the goal-line and right behind the foot of the hindmost player in the maul.

By understanding the concepts and rules surrounding the breakdown, we can look to coach the skills that are most effective during this critical part of the game.

Chapter 7:
Understanding the body for developing players

Overview

In this chapter you will gain knowledge of the following:

- ☑ **How the body works**
- ☑ **How the body grows**
- ☑ **Common injuries and prevention strategies**

Background

There is a whole science behind how the body works; specifically there is a whole industry that supports the training, recovery and development of rugby players.

A fundamental understanding of the body's energy system, and how it grows after exercise, will greatly assist the player in his understanding, and therefore inform him on selecting supplements to support his development if he wishes.

How the body works

If you are a scientist, or an expert in nutrition, you may understand the difference between Non-oxidative

(Anaerobic) and Oxidative (Aerobic) systems, but what do these terms really mean?

Non-oxidative (without oxygen) supplies rely on using stored resources known as adenosine triphosphate (ATP), phosphocreatine (PC), and the production of lactic acid (LA) and do not go into using oxygen to produce more energy. With oxidative (with oxygen), the body uses oxygen to aid in energy production through what is called the Krebs cycle. This whole process is called oxidation phosphorylation. The standard energy of all human motion is the release of energy. Therefore, replenishment of ATP or the removal and/or dissipation of the waste products associated with maintaining our ATP supplies are what happens inside our bodies when we play sports.

A trained rugby player knows how the system works and, as such, knows how to replenish the ATP that is being used. The three major components: ATP/PC, LA and oxidative have the ability to support activities of varying intensities and durations.

All athletes have the ability to produce power and work intensities that exceed their ability to resynthesize ATP. For example, even in a 100m sprint on the track, the athlete slows down due to fatigue. Similarly, in a series of five lineout jumps or explosive scrums, power output drops.

The stages of energy usage in the body

Physiologists have devised a method to look at the energy expenditures of different sports.

The first phase is called the ATP- PC system. ATP (Adenosine Triphosphate) is stored in all cells, particularly muscles. In a sense, it is free energy because the body stores ATP to make it available for immediate use, however, you can only use it once and it needs recovery time to restore. The ATP system is great for short and quick activities because it only lasts for about five seconds and is used in activities like 10-meter sprints.

When ATP is used it breaks down into adenosine diphosphate (ADP). ADP then can combine with phosphocreatine (PC) to make more ATP, but only for a short period of time, around 5-20 seconds. This system requires some recovery time as well. It takes about 25-30 seconds to regain about half of the phosphocreatine stores. These two systems combine for activities like 200m sprints and sports where short intermittent bursts of activity are required, for example, basketball, hockey, and rugby.

The next major phase is called the lactic (LA) system. After the 20 seconds of the ATP-PC system, the body requires another ingredient, muscle glycogen (glucose) to be added to continue.

This system begins when phosphocreatine stores are depleted. Lactic acid (or lactate) comes from the breakdown of the glucose released from the muscles. One of the outcomes of this breakdown is that positive Hydrogen ions are expelled which accumulate in the muscles and causes them to fatigue.

The lactic system is used in a number of sports that do repeat sprinting or high-energy activities, such as rugby, sprint cycling, 100m swim, and 400 meter sprints in athletics.

Training can therefore be designed to help the rugby player improve their tolerance to the buildup of the positive hydrogen ions. Training sessions of intense training, lasting from 25 to 45 seconds, with rest ranging from 20 seconds to three minutes.

The third system is the Oxidative phase. In this phase, as the term indicates, you are using oxygen to fuel the breakdown of carbohydrates first, free fatty acids second and if the exercise continues long enough - protein. Whereas, the previous systems have related to higher intensity work (or power) the aerobic system is more of moderate or low-intensity work, but of longer duration.

The oxidative system should be developed to aid in the lactic system. The development of the aerobic system aids in lactate removal, so that the athlete can tolerate more lactate. Training to develop this system consists of the traditional long runs, but can also have repeats of shorter distances of low intensity with reduced rest (20 x 200m with 30-second rest).

How the body grows

When we talk about training it can be simplified to three stages: stress, recovery, and adaptation. As a player, the challenge is to work the body (stress) through training, take a period of recovery (rest) and then allow the improvement to happen (adaption).

- **Stress** – Getting the body to work
- **Recovery** – Letting the body recover
- **Adaption** – Enabling the body to grow

Through adaptation, the rugby player can gradually develop the capability to handle more training or training with more intensity. As a player, you need to manipulate combinations of training frequency (how often you train), training intensity (how hard you train), and training duration (how long you train).

Another key factor is how the training you are doing relates to your playing standard and position. Physiologists call this Specific Adaptations to Imposed Demands (SAID).

Stress stage

Chapter 3 of this book contains a number of exercises designed to specifically stress the body of a rugby player. Chapter 5 of this book identifies the specific exercise for this specific playing position on the rugby field. Use these exercises and the knowledge of the ATP-CP energy system to design your own specific workout that will help you develop as a rugby player.

Rest stage

Essentially the rest stage should start with warming down of the body using the same exercises prior to the stress stage.

Next comes rehydration. This depends on your sweat rate, but on average, a player will cover between 8 and 12 kilometers a game. To work out how much you need to drink to rehydrate it is best to weigh yourself before and after training. If you lose 1.5 kg in sweat you should replace 1.2-1.5 times that amount. That means slowly consuming between 1.8 to 2.25 liters of fluid at the end of each training session or match.

Adaptation stage

In response to any form of movement, the body undergoes a multitude of adaptations, both acute (sudden, temporary changes in body function caused by physical exertion are termed acute), and chronic (adaptations that enable the body to respond more favourably to subsequent training sessions). The four key adaptions that enable athletes to perform better are the lungs, heart, muscles and, bones.

- **The lungs** - The lungs become more adept at ventilating larger volumes of air during intense physical exertion.
- **The heart** - The main heart adaptation is an increase in size, as it works to accommodate a greater cardiac output from session to session.
- **The muscles** - An aerobically trained muscle has more capillaries and mitochondria leading to a greater capacity to store fuel.
- **The bones** - The skeletal system involves the process of re-modelling (when cells called osteoclasts break down old bone as cells called osteoblasts replace it with new tissue to make it denser and stronger).

Common injuries and prevention strategies

Rugby players wear very little, if any, protective equipment, and their body is exposed to all of those hard hits. Studies have shown that injuries are the most common reason for players to quit playing rugby. Successive injuries over time can lead to long-term effects. Injuries common to rugby include muscle strains, knee sprains, contusions, hip dislocations, and facial injury.

Most Common Rugby Injuries

There are many injuries that can take place during the course of a game, the most common ones are identified below:

- **Muscle Strain** - When competing in rugby or practicing for competition, the muscles are stressed and stretched repeatedly. A hard-driving scrum or a move to evade a defender can place the muscles at risk of tearing. When the muscle tears it becomes weaker, pain and tenderness set in, and some slight swelling and bruising may occur. A minor strain will respond to ice, rest, and allow a return to full activity within one to two weeks.

- **Knee Sprain** - Any of the ligaments in the knee are subject to sprain in a hard-hitting rugby game. The most common sprains include the anterior cruciate ligament (ACL) and the medial collateral ligament (MCL.) The ACL is often torn when the foot and lower leg are planted, but the upper leg rotates. The MCL is commonly sprained by contact from another player on the outside of the knee. The severity of the sprain is determined by the amount of tearing present in the ligament, with the worst being a complete rupture. Minor sprains may take two to

77

three weeks for recovery, while a total tear may take eight weeks. Ice, and immobilization will help with recovery.

- **Bruises and Contusions** - As with any contact sport, bruises and contusions are very common in rugby. Players are being impacted in many directions, and those hard-hits result in blood vessels under the skin rupturing which causes swelling, pain, discoloration, and tenderness. Most contusions can be treated with ice. Deeper contusions in the muscle tissue may require rest and a gradual return to

Injury prevention strategies

To compete in the modern game of rugby a rugby player should develop a natural protective layering (musculature) and be strong enough to withstand the physical impacts of the game.

Practicing the game and becoming proficient in the skills of rugby condition the body when delivering a tackle, or taking one, which will help the player avoid some of the most common injuries in rugby.

Use of the minimal protective equipment such as a mouth guard would help shield the body from some of the usual injuries encountered in a game or during practice.

Strength training will help build protective muscle tissue over the bones and joints and will help keep the body healthy for games and speed recovery should an injury occur.

Flexibility is vital to condition the body to cope when it is twisted and contorted at different angles during tackles or when avoiding a defender, so a good flexibility routine is essential.

The top three rugby stretches

Stretching is one of the most under-utilized techniques for improving athletic performance, preventing sports injury, and properly rehabilitating sprain and strain injury. Don't make the mistake of thinking that something as simple as stretching won't be useful. The following three essential stretching exercises are very beneficial for rugby players.

- **Reaching-up shoulder stretch** - Place one hand behind your back and then reach up between your shoulder blades.

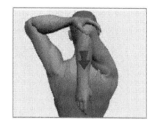

- **Lying knee roll-over stretch** - While lying on your back, bend your knees and let them fall to one side. Keep your arms out to the side and let your back and hips rotate with your knees.

- **Kneeling Quad Stretch** - Kneel on one foot and the other knee. If needed, hold on to something to keep your balance and then push your hips forward.

Chapter 8:
Natural windows for player development

Overview

In this chapter you will gain knowledge of the following:

- ☑ **Development windows**
- ☑ **Anatomical adaption**

Background

Developing players, who are committed to their own success, continually look to improve themselves. Whether it be developing their attacking, defensive, physical or mental conditioning, or working on the core essentials of positional specific excellence, they desire to be the very best they can be.

As humans, we are continually learning and developing new skills through life experiences. There are, however, some extraordinary development windows during the younger years of five to seventeen whereby the developing rugby player can accelerate the skills needed for exceptional rugby.

Development windows

Strength and conditioning is an absolutely essential part of developing a competent player in the sport of rugby union.

However, to progress, the player, family, coach and support network must understand the 'windows' of development within the young athlete.

- **Skills window** – This occurs between the approximate ages of 8 to 11 for girls and 9 to 12 years of age for boys.
- **Speed window** - During the growth spurt for boys it is important for coaches to understand the Long Term Player Development Pathway (FTPDP) if they are to successfully take advantage of opportunities for skill and fitness development and maintain the players commitment to the sport they love.

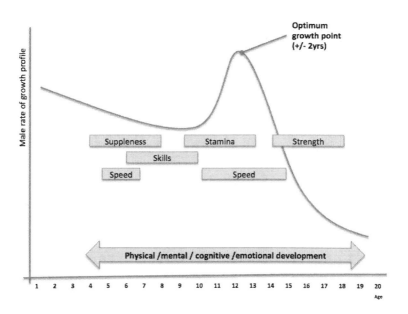

There is ample evidence showing that children and teenagers can improve in strength (Falk and Tenembaum, 1996, Payne et al., 1997), anaerobic fitness (Tolfrey, 2007) and aerobic fitness (Baquet et al., 2003) as well as speed, balance and stability (Gilligan et al., 2005). Further, resistance training, when completed under the qualified supervision of an adult, is safe, and gains can be made by children as young as 8 to 10 years of age (Payne et al., 1997, Falk and Tenembaum, 1996).

Given the possibilities for improved general fitness within developing players, it is important not to assume that scaled-down adult program are appropriate.

The process of growth and development, which occurs throughout the pre-teenage and teenage years, needs to be understood so that appropriate development of a player is managed in a safe, progressive and enjoyable manner.

Long Term Player Development Pathway (LTPDP)

As regards the adult game, we are aware of the importance of ensuring that the player is developed and prepared to play in a periodised and progressive manner. The latter stages of the Long Term Player Development Pathway (LTPDP), including the "Learn to Compete" and "Train to Win" stages, provide guidelines for the strength and conditioning coach at the adult game level.

Active Sport	FUN	Learning to Train	Training to Train	Training to Compete	Training to Win	Active for Life
Ages 0-6	Ages 6-9	Ages 8-11	Ages 11-15	Ages 15-21	Ages 19+	

Functional screening is an effective method of observing movement imbalances within a player during the "Training to Train" and "Training to Compete "windows which, if corrected early, can improve the player's enjoyment within the game and increase the duration they can remain in the "Training to Win" phase.

Chapter 9:
Recognition pathways for developing players

Overview

In this chapter you will gain knowledge of the following:

- ☑ **Player development pathways**
- ☑ **Competency framework**

Player development pathways

There are many ways for a young rugby player to be recognised at an elite level, and official pathways do exist to help identify and develop those players at club and regional levels.

Whereas it is fully understood that different kids develop at different ages, it is beneficial for the young athlete to understand the pathways early so they can get access to the higher levels of coaching needed and to get on the "rugby radar".

Those "rugby radars" can be very subjective, especially at the early stages of development, and that is why the core disciplines of catch and pass, tackling, and breakdown skills need to be continuously developed and honed through those development years.

Australian Rugby Union development pathway

This is the current publicised pathways for developing rugby players in Australia (2017).

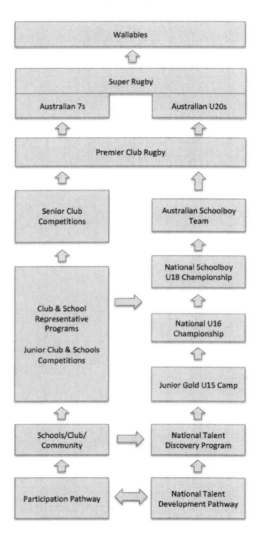

New Zealand 15 aside development pathway

This is the current publicised junior pathways for developing rugby players in New Zealand (2017).

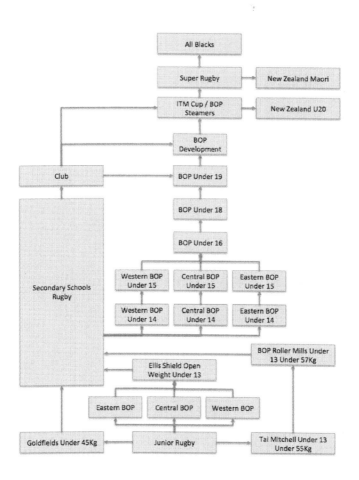

USA Rugby development pathway

This is the current publicised junior pathways for developing rugby players in America (2017).

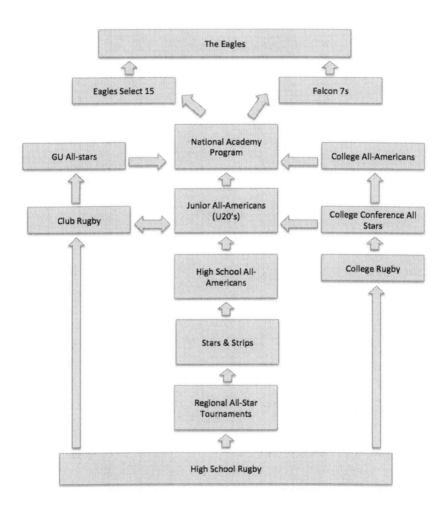

English Rugby Union development pathway

This is the current publicised junior pathways for developing rugby players in England (2017).

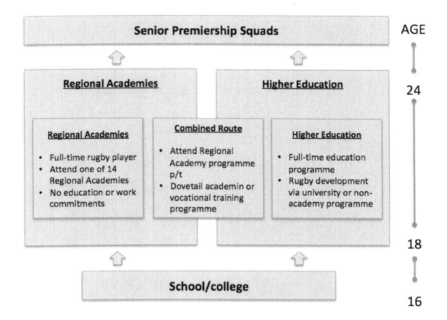

Welsh Rugby Union development pathway

This is the current publicised junior pathways for developing rugby players in Wales (2017).

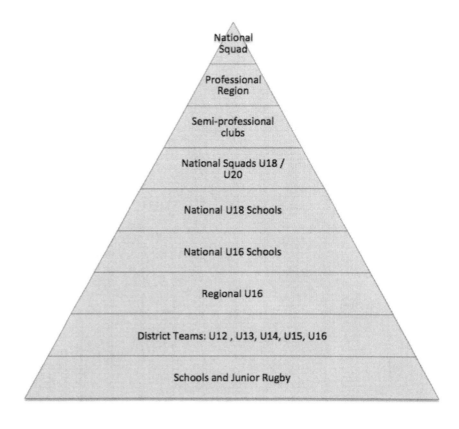

National Squad

Professional Region

Semi-professional clubs

National Squads U18 / U20

National U18 Schools

National U16 Schools

Regional U16

District Teams: U12 , U13, U14, U15, U16

Schools and Junior Rugby

Competency framework

Many players, coaches and supportive family members spend a lot of time and effort trying to identify their development route to becoming a professional rugby player. Some will even go as far as to change region, jobs and even countries in pursuit of development paths that meet their needs. Sometimes getting recognised by the right development officer or national scout is a matter of luck and timing, however that just gets you started.

Develop A Player has developed a free professional player profile at www.developaplayer.com where players can record and promote their rugby successes. Additionally all developing players from ages six through to seniors can get access and record their competency development at each age and against each position thereby allowing them to become the architect of their own development success.

Attacking competency framework

Skill	Description	Level 1	Level 2	Level 3
Scrum	Scrummaging ability in specific position.	Understands role on the pitch in attack.	Performs well at set pieces to disrupt opposition.	Leads set pieces and is effective at disrupting opposition ball.
Lineout	Lineout ability in specific position.	Understands role on the pitch in attack.	Performs well at set pieces and in broken play.	Leads lineouts and is effective at attacking plays.
Restarts	Ability to be effective in restarts.	Understands restart concepts of attack.	Can read restart positioning and adapts.	Mastery in restart situations.
Breakdown	Ability to be effective at the breakdown.	Understands the basics of the breakdown.	Contributes at the breakdown and is effective.	Expert at the breakdown in attack.

Open Play	**Ability to attack in open play.**	Understands the basics of attack.	Effective in attack with the ball.	Effective in attack with or without the ball.
Catch and Pass	**Ability to catch and pass the ball.**	Can catch and pass the ball.	Effective in catch and pass.	Effective in all types of catch and pass.
Kicking	**Ability to kick.**	Can kick the ball effectively.	Effective in all aspects of kicking attack.	Mastery in kicking ability in attack.
Shapes and Structures	**Attacking shapes and structures.**	Understands basic shapes and structures.	Understands where to use shapes and structures.	Can adapt shapes and structures to game situations.

Field Positioning	Understands Field segmentation.	Understands different parts of the field	Understand parts of the field and what plays to use.	Mastery in field movement and appropriate plays

Defensive competency framework

Skill	Description	Level 1	Level 2	Level 3
Scrum	Scrummaging ability in specific position.	Understands role when the opposition has the ball.	Understands role when the opposition has the ball and can have an impact	Leads set pieces and has an impact on the opposition
Lineout	Lineout ability in specific position.	Understands role when the opposition has the ball.	Understands role when the opposition has the ball and can have an impact	Leads the lineout and has an impact on the opposition
Restarts	Ability to be effective in restarts.	Understands restart concepts of defence.	Can read restart positioning and adapts.	Mastery in restart situations.

Breakdown	Ability to be effective at the breakdown.	Understands the basics of the breakdown.	Contributes at the breakdown in defence	Expert at the breakdown and can force turn-overs
Open Play	Ability to attack in open play.	Understands the basics of defence in open play.	Effective in open play defence.	Effective in open play defence and has an impact on the oppositions attack capability
Kicking	Ability to kick.	Understands different parts of the field while in defence	Understands defensive policies in defending kicks.	Mastery in field defence and adapts to opposition kicks.
Shapes and Structures	Attacking shapes and structures.	Understands the basic rules of defensive shapes and structures	Understands the defensive shapes and structures and can adapt	Has a deep understanding of defensive shapes and structures and can influence the attacking options.

Field Positioning	**Understands Field segmentation.**	Understands role on the pitch in defence.	Understands and anticipates field positioning in defence	Understands, adapts and has an impact of the attacking ability of a team by defensive field positioning.
Rules of the Game	**Understanding of the rules.**	Understands role on the pitch in defence.	Has a good understanding of all the defensive rules of the game.	Has a deep understanding of the defensive rules of the game
Scrum	**Scrummaging ability in specific position.**	Understands role when the opposition has the ball.	Understands role when the opposition has the ball and can have an impact	Leads set pieces and has an impact on the opposition

97

Physical conditioning competency framework

Skill	Description	Level 1	Level 2	Level 3
Scrum	Scrummaging conditioning in specific position.	Has the core conditioning to perform in the role.	Has developed good conditioning to perform well in the role.	Has developed advanced conditioning to perform exceptionally in the role.
Lineout	Lineout conditioning in specific position.	Has the core conditioning to perform in the role.	Has developed good conditioning to perform well in the role.	Has developed advanced conditioning to perform exceptionally in the role.
Breakdown	Conditioning to be effective at the breakdown.	Has the core conditioning to be effective at the breakdown.	Has the core conditioning to impact the breakdown.	Has the core conditioning to significantly impact the breakdown

Open Play	**Conditioning for open play.**	Has the core conditioning to perform in open play.	Has the conditioning to be effective in open play.	Has developed advanced conditioning for open play rugby.
Catch and Pass	**Conditioning for catch and pass.**	Has the core conditioning to effectively catch and pass.	Has the conditioning to be effective in catch and pass.	Has developed advanced conditioning for catch and pass skills.

99

Mental conditioning competency framework

Skill	Description	Level 1	Level 2	Level 3
Set piece	Mental conditioning for set piece rugby.	Has the core mental conditioning for set piece rugby.	Has developed good mental conditioning for set piece rugby.	Has developed advanced mental conditioning for set piece rugby.
Catch and Pass	Mental conditioning Catch and Pass.	Has the core mental conditioning to perform catch and pass	Has developed good mental conditioning for advanced catch and pass.	Has developed advanced mental conditioning for excellent catch and pass skills under pressure
Breakdown	Mental conditioning for breakdown.	Has the core mental conditioning to perform at the breakdown.	Has developed good mental conditioning to perform at the breakdown.	Has developed advanced mental conditioning to perform at the breakdown.
Open Play	Mental conditioning for open play.	Has the core mental conditioning to perform in the role.	Has the mental conditioning to be effective in open play.	Has developed advanced mental conditioning for open play.

100

Courage to Win	Mental conditioning to win.	Understands mental visualization.	Can utilise effective mental imagery.	Mastery at effective mental imagery.

101

Chapter 10:
Develop A Player developmental portal

Overview

In this chapter you will gain knowledge of the following:

- ☑ **Our purpose**
- ☑ **Free professional player profile for Number 8 (No.8)**

Our purpose

Develop A Player was established with a specific purpose, which was to remove the participation barrier for all players wanting to take part in the sport of rugby union.

To set up your FREE Professional Player Profile you just need to go to: **www.developaplayer.com**

Free professional player profile for a Number 8

- **Step 1** – Click on Player Zone Registration to get this screen.
- **Step 2** – Enter a valid e-mail address and create a password.
- **Step 3** – Enter your name, Date of Birth and nationality.
- **Step 4** – Upload a profile picture (.jpeg).
- **Step 5** – Enter your player information.
- **Step 6** – Read and accept the terms and conditions and privacy policy.
- **Step 7** – Click register.

You will receive a one-time password in your e-mail inbox. Enter that code into the confirmation screen and then you're all done.

Welcome to Develop A Player.

References and acknowledgements

Balyi and Way, 2005

Falk and Tenembaum, 1996, Payne et al. 1997

Tolfrey, 2007

Baquet et al. 2003

Gilligan et al. 2005.

Payne et al. 1997, Falk and Tenembaum, 1996.

Develop A Player, 2012

ARU, 2015

www.developaplayer.com

Printed in Great Britain
by Amazon